The Poetics of Episteme-art

Adão Vieira de Faria

THE POETICS OF EPISTEME-ART

1st Edition
POD

KBR
Greenville
2015

Publisher **Noga Sklar**
Translation **Noga Sklar**
Text edition **Alan Sklar**
Cover design **KBR**
Cover illustration **based on *Bicycle Wheel*, ready-made scultpture by Marcel Duchamp, 1913**

Title of the original in Portuguese: *Poética da Episteme-Arte*
Copyright © 2012 *Adão Vieira de Faria*
All rights reserved.

ISBN: 978-1-944608-02-6
ISBN: 978-1-944608-03-3 (E-book)

KBR Digital Publishers LLC.
www.kbrdigital.com
www.facebook.com/kbrdigital
contact@kbrdigital.com

Greenville - SC
1|864|373.4528

PHI001000 - Philosophy / Aesthetics

Adão Vieira de Faria was born in 1954, in the Lagoa Seca farm in Itumbiara, Goiás, Brazil. In 1975, after completing high school in Goiânia, he moved to Ouro Preto, where he graduated in engineering from UFOP, while, at the same time, starting his art studies. After an unfinished specialization in COPPE, UFRJ, he settled in Ipatinga, Minas Gerais, in 1980. Summing up his productive years in engineering and theater, he founded the Boca de Cena theatre company in 1983, in which, after devoting 10 years to classical ballet with the Bolshoi, under the guidance of dancer and choreographer Zélia Olguin, he deepened his studies of drama, music and science. With Boca de Cena he produced multimedia pieces, acting as an actor, director, author, costume designer and set designer in more than 30 plays. He's been a professor of architecture and engineering at the Centro Universitário do Leste de Minas since 2000. In 2007 he obtained his master's degree in engineering from UFMG.

Email: avdefaria@uol.com.br

TABLE OF CONTENTS

Acknowledgment • 9
About The Summary • 13
About the Art of Poetry • 15
About Myth, Logos and the Tragic, in Art and Creation • 25
About Epistemology as the Art of Poetry • 35
About the Crisis of Utopias • 49
About the Post-Crisis of Utopias • 65
About the Bibliographic References • 91

Acknowledgment

Noga, we have only one word for your editing job: "INCREDIBLE!"

Dum cupit Empedocles, ardentem
frigidus Aetnam insiluit.

Horatio, *Ars Poetica - Epistula ad Pisones (465)¹*

---
1 Trigale, D. *A arte poética de Horácio.*

About The Summary

The concepts of Mimesis and Verisimilitude, described by Aristotle in his *Poetics*, still permeate the academic and artistic worlds filled with mistakes that are derived from vitiated and tendentious translations. When the dust and absurdities that time helps to conceal are swept away, Plato's main disciple is revealed to be more contemporary than many would like to acknowledge. His analytical criteria to deal with tragic poetry are so broad and sophisticated, that it is possible to point out elements of several disciplines contained in them.

The act of creating, in Art as well as in any other field, is always the result of a "Tragic" tension between the conscious, *self-conscious* doing, and the unconscious, *non-self-*

conscious doing. Thus, it is possible to break any barrier that can still hinder the possibility of seeing Art as Science and vice-versa. Creation is always a process, not something exclusive to the "Enlightened." "Possibilities," even if ambiguous — like in Stochastic, Quantum or continuous functions — or "Pseudo-exacts" — as in the equations of Quantum Mechanics — can be treated as metaphors.

The fall of utopias has only reinforced the solitude imposed by our space-time awareness and the resulting *a priori* need for a Creator, ideally extant from our Self, even in the age of Relativity and Quantum aesthetics. This fear of ours, which is reason itself, of facing the flow of life's unpredictability, will very likely demand Utopias — as the one our country presently witnesses, that of "Social Inclusion" and "Socially Engaged Art" — that will unfold in increasingly sophisticated self-deceits. We have only one alternative: in order to shorten the road to nowhere, or Self, "Fine Art" must give way to "Episteme-Art."

About the Art of Poetry

Aristotle, in an attempt to bring to his students and perhaps to himself an understanding of the elements that form artistic expression and Art itself, elaborated one of his most notorious classroom notes, that has reached modern day as *The Art of Poetry*.[2] It has been translated in nearly every language. The novelty of the subject and the distance in time led to translations that were either distorted or laden with the translators' assumptions.

It is very likely that the great philosopher had made use of Theatrical Art in his argumentations, not only for its widespread acceptance and social weight at the time, but

---

2 Aristóteles. *Poética*, Portuguese translation by Jaime Bruna.

also for being a trans-disciplinary art. Even in its simplest form, Theater is the result of the interpretation of a text or a script, singing, music, stage design, visual arts, costume design and, in the last instance — one of its greatest peculiarities — the use of Man himself as a means of expression. This observation intends to alert sectarians about the dimensions of the work upon which we are commenting.

We must remember that long before Aristotle music had already been de-mystified by Pythagoras and his followers with the creation of the Diatonic Scale, demonstrating that Art, to an extent, can be codified and documented in a first epistemological approach. We may infer that the "genius" of this man, who sketched the rudiments of Logic, attempted the same with Art as a whole, in this unique and monumental piece, perhaps the most widely read — *The Art of Poetry*.

Art, until then inhabiting the world of Shamans and Oracles, starts to be dealt intelligently, seen in the light of the Dialectic. Aristotle demonstrates that artistic expression is the result of an ordered and logical action, "sensible reason," in search of a Mimetic and feasible portrait of life or life events. The "primary configuration" of this portrait with one or many functional possibilities, ambiguous as they are, will be resolved as Art.

Recently, the academic and philosopher Michael Davis[3] showed that the term "Verisimilitude" is less Christian and more scientific than the Renaissance translators believed. With Davis, this term travels to the English language as "likely," and could also be translated as "Possibility," namely that which suggests or allows for Intelligibility, regardless of its quantum, fractal or continuous nature. The tradition within the Academy always defines the term "Verisimilitude" as something related or referring to the *Truth*, if not considered as truth itself, and therefore heavy with Christian dualism and a late Platonism.

Davis, when discussing the structure of Action, introduces Tragedy as one of the most perfect of poetic manifestations, given that, more than any other artistic manifestation, it embodies quite well the two elements of human endeavor or the creation of Poetry: the conscious doing, *self-conscious*, and the unconscious doing, *non-self-conscious*. These two aspects of action may be defined as: the part of the Spectator, responsible for intelligibility and the part of the Actor, responsible for dealing with uncertainty, freedom and frankness. The combination of those in a given poem implies their necessary combination in human action.

The concept of Metaphor itself, when

---

3 Davis, M. *The Poetry of Philosophy on Aristotle's Poetics.*

analyzed and reexamined in light of Aristotle's *Poetics*, acquires a greater consistency, not to mention Logic. Paul Ricoeur[4] suggests in his writings that the Metaphor may be understood as a configurator of the possibilities of artistic action, or what we may call the condensation of feasible Mimesis.

In Ricoeur, paradoxically, Mimesis and Metaphor submit themselves to reality as they fabulously depart from it as well: they magnify human actions by transfiguring them, or by ideally representing them. The poet Fernando Pessoa, in *A Tabacaria;* Sophocles, in *Oedipus Rex*; Homer, in *The Odyssey*; Rodin, with "The Kiss"; and Van Gogh, with "The mailman" are some of the ones who best understood it.

In the Stagiritis, Ernesto Grassi[5] observes, Mimesis has distanced itself from the idea of a Primeval and Holy Truth, like his master Plato preached, and is revealed in the praxis of the merely human and possible accomplishment as an autonomous entity. Grassi starts with the affirmation that the Ontological character of Beauty and Art, present in Antiquity, can help in the understanding of some of the currents in contemporary thought that regard their manifestations as

---

4 Ricoeur, P. *La Methaphore vive*.
5 Grassi, E. *Arte como antiarte*.

original forms imbued with metaphysical values, as opposed to the conception of Art in the Modern Age, born in the Renaissance, that grants autonomy to Beauty and assigns to a particular discipline, Aesthetics, the responsibility for clarifying its essence.

According to Luiz Costa Lima,[6] in Aristotle, Mimesis stops being a shadow of Platonic truth and reaches the conception of Organism, an autonomous entity that shares the laws which govern the material cosmos of *Physis*. In other words, a participatory element of Concrete Existence, a *dynamis* potentiality that explodes as an *Ergon* product.

Lima claims that Mimetic discourse is the discourse of a signifier in search of a signification, which is assigned both by the author and — even mainly — by the recipient. In fewer words: in the effective reality of the Mimetic product, that is to say, in its circulation, a synthesis of similitude and differentiation is achieved.

Some artists, especially those who believe themselves to be unique beings —even seen as Illuminated, for that is how their followers and admirers have averred — have dared to lucidly control the possibilities of the Mimesis. That was the case of Jorge Luis Borges, for whom fiction is *anti-physis*,

---

6 Lima, L. *O Controle do Imaginário*.

non-mimetic, a function of life, regarded as a nightmare. Amplifying the understanding of Mimesis as described in the *Poetics*, Lima demonstrates that the irrespirable Borgesian production is ruled by the same laws that the Mimesis is subject to, as an example of what occurs with the Mimesis of Modernity, or "Mimesis of Production," characterized by the lack of internal organization in the text, simultaneous to the dis-socialization of representations.

In his essay "The Nature of Lyricism," José Guilherme Melquior[7] retrieves from the *Poetics* original entirety the idea of Aristotelian Mimesis: the "representation of something external and the inner settings of verbal and thematic elements." Melquior points out in this essay the cleverness with which Aristotle links poetry to reality and, at the same time, postulates the autonomy of the Aesthetic Sphere, given the constraints of the external world.

To those who insist on rendering art as a portrait of the unique, that is, historians and non-creators, or fabulators — and there are many — especially in the field of dance and video-dance; to those who even without understanding the concept of Mimesis deny it, using the aesthetics of realism as a

---

7 Melquior, J. *A Astúcia da Mimese.*

premise, as occurred with the Realist School circa 1830; to those who deny Art as an intelligent process, as the illuminated Christians of the Beat Generation intended, circa 1950, I call for the resurrection of those who already died, thus allowing them to review the concept of Mimesis and Myth; and to those who are still alive, and insist on calling themselves illuminated, let them all be crucified, urgently.

Melquior demonstrates that the artists from the Realist School conceived their works as a sensible mirror of reality, of a factual and empirical layer of historic process, and even so, insisted on practicing Mimesis, for an empiric-historical reference that nurtures realism is not the only form of reality, even in the case of a literary narrative.

Lígia Militz,[8] in her analysis of Mimesis and Verisimilitude described in the *Poetics*, makes the following conceptual propositions that presently concern us: Mimetic construction is presided over by a fundamental criterion, Verisimilitude; Verisimilitude situates Mimesis in the unlimited frontier of the possible; the Possible, and not the Truthful, is the thematic goal of Mimesis; the possible is in the field of probabilities, but it should

---

8 Costa, L. M. *A Poética de Aristóteles - Mimese/ Verossimilhança*.

be logical, causal and necessary, and regulate the actions of the Myth; everything is feasible in Mimesis, even the infeasible, as long as it has motivation, pretending to be tractable; Myth is taken for Mimesis, being the ability to compose a Myth, to represent Actions, what defines a man as a poet.

A work like *Don Quixote* would hardly be possible without a previous knowledge of the concept of feasible Mimesis, delineated by Aristotle based on works such as Homer's *The Iliad* and *The Odyssey*, Sophocles' *King Oedipus* and the monumental sculptures of Phidias. Even the great and respectable Erasmus of Rotterdam,[9] of whom Cervantes was a follower, could never have written one of his most influential works on the world of Arts and Creation, *The Praise of Folly*, without an acknowledgment of Aristotle's writings.

After the transubstantiation of Aristotle's *Poetics* by Michael Davis and Lígia Militz, it is hard not to highlight how much this work was fundamental in the construction of the aesthetics of Schopenhauer and his admirer, Friedrich Wilhelm Nietzsche. Even a less knowledgeable reader may realize that the Nietzschean concept of Superman, or *Übermensch*,[10] is nothing but a re-reading of

---

9 Rotterdam, E. *The Praise of Folly*.
10 Nietzsche, F. *Thus Spoke Zarathustra*.

Homer's *Odyssey*, plus the Aristotelian proposal of lucidity in the logical understanding of poetic creation. With some poetic license I am able to infer that the great Nietzsche, who like Erasmus read and wrote Greek, always despised the Christian translations of the *Poetics* when assembling his Aesthetics, based upon the concept of Dionysus and Apollo.

Bertolt Brecht himself, the preeminent playwright of the great Age of Utopias, seemingly did nothing but re-read Aristotle's *Poetics*, re-name a few things in his own way and propose what was very clearly described in the original. The Brechtian "concept of distancing," or *Verfremdungseffekt*, known as "V-effect" in his epic theater, was already used by the chorus in Greek plays and was noted in the *Poetics*. What Brecht did was broaden the analytical, critical and distancing role of the Greek chorus throughout the entire play, attempting to teach the audience to think and to avoid a catharsis that would add nothing to a socially engaged individual. Aristotle's moralism, so criticized by Nietzsche, comes in part from his role as an educator in a society based on the Myth of the Hero; or, maybe, from projecting onto Aristotle the figure of his father, a Protestant minister.

Guimarães Rosa,[11] in his unquestionable erudition — said to even read ancient Greek — practically repeats, with his hero Riobaldo, a Brazilian *Odyssey*, going as far as redefining in his own way the concept of feasible Mimesis with the sentence: "Our lives go on from one mistake to another, like a story that makes no sense for lack of seriousness and joy. Life should be as it is in the theater, each of us complete playing his role, his part, with the greatest pleasure." Mark Twain,[12] in his infamous observation, wrote something similar: "Truth is stranger than Fiction, but it is because Fiction is obliged to stick to possibilities; Truth isn't."

---

11 Rosa, J. *Grande Sertão: Veredas.*
12 Twain, M. *Pudd'nhead Wilson and Those Extraordinary Twins.*

About Myth, Logos and the Tragic, in Art and Creation

The concept of Myth adopted in the *Poetics* can and must be expanded. Before we proceed, let us start by reviewing how the linguist Antonio Houaiss[13] defines the words "Logos" and "Myth" as philosophic rubrics that correlate, thus making our proposal easier.

Logos: for Heraclitus of Ephesus, in the 5th century before Christ; an harmonic ensemble of laws, regularities and connections that command the Universe, forming a cosmic omnipresent intelligence that comes full

---
13 Houaiss, A. *Dicionário Eletrônico*.

circle in human thought; by extension, in religion, as in the Gospel of John: God the Creator and his son Jesus Christ, who can be understood as the embodiment in the world of the power and the absolute wisdom of Divine Reason. This term chosen by the Evangelist derives from the wide philosophical propagation of the word in the Hellenic world.

Etymology: from the Greek "λόγος" or "lógos" or language, proposition, definition; word; notion; reason; common sense; motif; judgment; opinion; estimation, value that is attributed; explanation; Divine Reason.

Myth: fantastic tale originating from oral tradition, usually enacted by beings who embody, in a symbolic form, the forces of nature and the general aspects of the human condition; legend, fable, mythology; allegorical exposition of any idea, doctrine or philosophical theory; fable, allegory; and by extension, the mental construction of something idealized, with no empirical proof; idea, stereotype.

Etymology: from the Greek "μυθος" or "mûthos," fable, report, speech, word.

Tragic: to deal with this word, we shall consider the study of Peter Szondi,[14] *An Es-*

---

14 Szondi, P. *An Essay on the Tragic.*

say on the Tragic. The *Poetics* gives consideration to tragedy, but not to the Tragic, which is here a term of utmost importance. According to Szondi, it is only since Schelling that a philosophy of the Tragic begins to exist. Aristotle, in the *Poetics*, discusses the elements of Tragic Art; his objective is the tragedy, not the idea of tragedy. Even when he goes beyond the concrete work of art, when he questions the origins and the effects of tragedy, the *Poetics* remains empirical in its doctrine of the Soul and in its considerations — the impulse of imitation as the origin of Art and the catharsis as the effect of tragedy.

Szondi compares commentaries of philosophical and aesthetic texts and writings of twelve authors from 1795 to 1915, in an attempt to frame a universal concept for the Tragic, *Tragisch*: Let us opt to describe only the definitions that concern us.

The Tragic in Schelling: the essence of tragedy is a real conflict between the freedom in the subject and his objective needs. This conflict does not end with the defeat of one or the other, but with the fact that in the end both appear as winners and losers alike. Thus, the Tragic is understood as a dialectical phenomenon; for non-differentiation between freedom and necessity is only possible when one pays the price for being simultaneously the winner and the loser — and vice-versa.

The Tragic in Goethe: the Tragic in its totality is based on irreconcilable opposition, *unausgleichbar*. The moment a reconciliation, *Ausgleichung*, appears or becomes possible, the Tragic disappears. Goethe could consider the act of departing the motivation of all Tragic situations, because he realized its dialectical structure. The farewell is unity whose only theme is division; it is proximity whose only perspective is distance; it aspires for the distance, even when it hates it; it is connection, consummated by its own separation, its death, as a departure.

The Tragic in Hegel: a dialectic submitted to Eticity, that is, the spirit in its moment of true spirit; a conflict between love and the world of law, as in Sophocles' *Antigone*.

The Tragic in Schopenhauer: the self-destruction and self-denial of human desire made manifest. Art is the tragic mirror of the world, since it is free from the objectives of such desire. Knowledge, which is deeply rooted in the desire itself and at its service, turns against it. Life, as the objective and the objectivity of this desire "is not worthy of the spectator's affection," driving him to resignation.

The Tragic in Hebbel: Tragic Art "annihilates the individual's life as a reaction to an idea," and thus "elevates itself above it." Because of that, Tragic Art is merely the "brilliant lightning of human consciousness, which cannot illuminate anything without destroying it." Therefore, in annihilation, Tragedy grants recognition to a meaning that is annihilated in knowledge itself. Hebbel's "pantragicity" culminates in the Tragedy of Tragic Art. In Hebbel, according to Szondi,[15] in a rationally insolvable trial that reminds us of Kafka, man is declared guilty in relation to a vital power that he does not know or understand. In Hegel's work, the Tragic hero, whose *pathos* unequivocally represents Eticity, incurs in guilt, not only towards other personifications of Eticity, but towards eticity itself.

The Tragic in Nietzsche: a God who experiments within himself the suffering of individuation. Art is no longer a perfect mirror, as in Schopenhauer, where the world of individuation expresses judgment over will; it is an indication that individuation represents "the primordial fundament of Evil" as much as the cheerful hope that the spell of individuation may be broken, and the feeling of a unity can be established.

---
15 Szondi, P. *An Essay on the Tragic*.

In Miguel de Cervantes's *Don Quixote*,[16] an individuation so expressive to the point of being mad, the totality barely allows him the right to be an individual without being the totality at the same time; it does not accept the limits of reality and, as a consequence, is turned virtual, and let us say, aesthetic. This mythical knight of Cervantes is, at the same time, a subject and a state of being — or love, as in *Antigone* -—, the totality and the individual, or a god who experiments the individuation within himself, as it seems to happen to all Tragic heroes, at least until Euripides.

We are all, so to speak, a leak in the flow of existence; the price of the individual's reintegration to his origins is entropic annihilation, or the Tragic. Entropy requires order to realize itself, and that is the big question, the great enigma of existence.

Inspired by Szondi's notes, I will at this point add some of my own. The Tragic is the confrontation between a being and the absolute loneliness of his return path to the totality, the process of his annihilation; it is also, in a way, the price of individuation, better yet, of the totality.

What we are living today, according to Szondi, in these days of Christian aegis, has

---

16 Cervantes Saavedra, M. *Don Quixote de La Mancha*.

been observed before by Calderón and also by Gryphius: "The force of total union, of the Christian promise of salvation, eliminates the tragic rupture." This might explain the near impossibility of performing Greek tragedies today without a psychological perspective, often a very shallow one. With the advent of a Christian aesthetic, the "third mask," Fear & Terror, has ascended to heaven, and to mere mortals, these renovated gods have left only the other two: Sadness & Compassion and Comedy & Joy. How can we get out of this mess? Going back to Ancient Greece, or to neo-anthropocentrism or, perhaps, to the knowledge and facing of death itself.

Without reverting to metaphysics, already being metaphysical, we can imagine the following possibility: the order that allows for the flow of life is of the same genre as the one that permits the flow of consciousness. The dialectical replication, copy or Mimesis, starts in the quantum randomness of the world or even in the *anti-physis*; it acquires the awareness that, grounded in the same dialectic, gropes the unknown; but tragically annihilates itself, fed only and exclusively by the synthesis Courage & Belief.

In order to make things easier, let us try to redefine Possibility, Logos, Myth and Tragic, in a way that is more specific to this essay:

> ***Possibility***: *what is intelligible, or the individuation's impulse to order.*
> ***Logos***: *all the possibilities.*
> ***Tragic***: *the tension between desire and duty, or between the individuation that is totality, and the totality itself.*
> ***Myth***: *the primary configuration of the possibility through the act of individuation.*

In this way, I maintain that Possibilities of every order permeate the Logos. In the flow and re-flow of the things of existence, order is a barrier that tries to halt the annihilation of a Possibility; back to the *black hole* where the unconscious lies and from where the singularity emerges, from which the Possibilities precipitate as Myths. "*Black hole*" should be understood as the abode of the unknown, nothing else. It is said that the unconscious is quantum and even structural, but let us leave that for another time. Natural selection is random, imposed by entropy and by a superb will to return everything and everyone back to its origins, thus elevating an action antithetical to order and finally allowing the existence of other Possibilities even more complex, stable and effectual against annihilation. Like the knots in a net, that get stronger as they are pushed and pulled, so does the mechanism of Mimesis appear:

as an efficient exit in the fight for the possibility of permanence, in the face of a world that melts even before it is completed. I Mimetize, therefore I think!

About Epistemology as the Art of Poetry

By analyzing the *Poetics*, Lígia Militz[17] concludes that Myth is intertwined with Mimesis as the ability to create Myth, to represent actions, what defines man as Poet. In the universe of Greek Paideia, it is very likely that the Poet was seen as one who creates, not merely produces lyrical poetry; and that Myth already had a larger expression, that of comprising every and any result of human Tragic & Action as well.

Subjectivity, or the Logos that feeds any creator/ created, is of the same genre, whether in Art, Rhetoric or Science. Any mythi-

---

17 Costa, L. M. *A Poética de Aristóteles - Mimese/ Verossimilhança*.

cized possibility, whether this Myth, exact or subjective as it may seem, an equation, a song, a musical score, a poem or any other creation, will always be the result of the Logos precipitation process through the action of the Tragic. This might put artists to enormous shame, especially those who consider themselves heralds of creation or enlightened beings, as is often the case.

The time has come for putting a stop to this trained man, a copyist, a repeater, sedentary and opportunistic. Our fate is to create possibilities: from the more subjective ones, whose purpose is but suggestion, sometimes weak as in some arts, to the concrete and utilitarian, as in equations, projects, sketches, etc. To accomplish that, we can only rely on courage and, in the worst case scenario, on trust and belief, in what it does not matter. Everything counts, provided that we attend to this terrible need: living.

With the triumphal rebirth of Greek thought, circa 1500, René Descartes[18] promotes an advance in Aristotelian logic, making the understanding of the world and its phenomena even easier. With his concept of function, filled with mathematics and philosophy, "*Cogito, ergo sum,*" he demonstrates that a possibility, or many,

---

18 Descartes, R. *Discourse on Method.*

is or will be able to, someday, be better understood and described by a logical function, which is nothing other than the epistemological expression of an applied dialectic, as we know, an offspring of the Greek rhetorical arts.

Even under the dominion of the Christian aesthetic of Good and Evil, Newton[19] finds or mythicizes the great *metaphor* of the movement of bodies, in his famous equation "F = ma," that is, *the resultant of "F" forces applied over a material point equals the product of its mass "m" by the acquired acceleration "a."* Nothing prevents us from imagining that Newton composed a poem, or found a possibility for the "becoming" of the falling of bodies, or, less Deleuzian, a verisimilitude for this falling. Not far from all of this, Miguel de Cervantes would give to the world his masterpiece *Don Quixote,* maybe the first modern novel, or what we may call a possibility for the becoming of man. Shakespeare's *Hamlet*, architect of humanness, baptizes Newton and Cervantes, and the Greeks are reborn to wake up the world.

It may seem daring and a bit reductionist, but it is possible to realize that, under the action of the Tragic, by way of Mimesis

---

[19] Newton, I. *Principia.*

and its intrinsic process, these creators tried to give shape to possibilities their intelligent brains had experimented with: the Word, embodying Myths that are feasible, therefore, possible. Being even bolder, I claim that they noticed and spread to the world important metaphors, full of *signifiers* in search of *signification*.

It is my contention that, at this point, I have lost all those readers who still believe that sensitivity disappears with the exercise of logic, by creating and suggesting quantum, even continuous or necessary possibilities, as some prefer. That being the case, in order to reinforce this escape and with my own permission, I put Heraclitus, Plato, Aristotle and Homer as absolute lords of the Art of Poetry — now, yesterday, today and forever an epistemologist, even if I am certain that those in traditional Academies will censor me.

With his *Poetics* of *Poetics*, Aristotle realized how to create a work that, more than lyrical, was a work of "conceptual art." We can define him as a "pre-conceptualist" or, perhaps, "post-conceptualist" artist. May Clement Greenberg, the New York arts critic who cared to systematize this art, forgive me. Let us look at things this way: it's been a long time since art as material objects dropped out of vogue, and Duchamp — with his *ready-mades* and his concept-wheel, which I now propose to be broken — is nothing but a media buffoon. Thus, we are compelled to recover the Tragic, to break all the "escape routes" and to face Paidea once more, without pre-conceived ideas.

The following text illustrates, in dramatic soliloquy, the indecision of a man in the face of his uncertainties and his desire to exist, or better yet, in order to exist. How to overcome oneself, to embody the Tragic and to propose some "Primal Possibility" — maybe even a different kind of "Original Sin," that, in the worst case scenario, might fill oneself with enthusiasm?

The First Soliloquy: "*I even know where the grapes are!*"

I will never write a text that will amount to anything; that will be really poignant and significant. Look, pay close attention! "My dream is to wander…." It is the most ridiculous thing I've ever heard. Figure it out! It was my intention to come up with beautiful lyrics, sung by the heroine in my ex-future text.

(The actor crumples sheets of paper on the floor and cries, in solitude.)

I'm half-alive. I live this lukewarm thing, drifting from the fear of living to the fear of dying. I envy my friends terribly. Everyone of them lives with such intensity, such excitement, they love really hard. I am this insipid thing, swallowed by the ordinary. Mediocrity. Domingos de Oliveira! This is my hero, yes, of whom I am unworthy of even pronouncing the name. Listen: "I, Domingos de Oliveira, am what my wives have made of me... ," why say anything else? Here is someone who has touched the divine. He looks tragedy in the eyes. He goes deeply without fear, extracts and drinks life's purest nectar. Vianinha was like this. So was Shakespeare. So was everyone who inspired us in life! So are most of my few friends. Just the other day I met one of them; he was profoundly beaten, not to say destroyed. The declared cause: the defeat of his soccer team. I was dying of envy! I had never seen such passion in a single person. I soon imagined how big his pleasure would be when this same team wins. I will never be like this! I'm a bankrupt project!

I even know where the grapes are, but I am not tall enough to reach them. Before, I believed my feelings to be pure self-pity. Perhaps due to the influence of a psychologist friend trying to cheer me up. Another bankrupt project, of course! Now I have no further doubts about being a worthless thing. Nothing but a number, something to help nature with the selection of its favorites. Now these are the ones deserving glory, the true heralds of creation. They possess a specialized antenna that anticipates and open the path for those who cowardly crawl. Women, as divas of creation, own a very specialized instinct to detect those who own the most tragic and vigorous sperm there is. They couldn't care less if it belongs to Hitler, Napoleon, Einstein or Brando. What matters in their choice is the ability of the chosen to inspire the world. Poor us, the ordinary! *All that is left to us is to try and make-believe we have an UTOPIA, adding value to the losers' old saying: "It's not whether you win or lose. It's how you play the game."*

(The actor gets another piece of paper from the floor and starts reading.)

My dream is to wander..."

It is not hard to realize that the character who just spelled out his tragic agony is, without a shadow of doubt, a regretful Christian. His great fight lies, in fact, in discovering how to forget the paradise his evangelized consciousness promised him, and walking with legs of his own towards the unknown, hidden behind his metaphysics — the comforting, unprecedented manger of his fear of facing the Tragic. How to solve this impasse? How to put all this into theater and art? How to abandon the dream of the promised heaven and make yourself Tragic? How to forget Hegel and his lucidity?

The heaven of the Hegelian aesthetic is scatological, and puts the human species at risk. There is nothing on earth that overcomes the satisfaction proposed by all these metaphysics of happiness — based on the idleness of celestial Eden, far above the Pantheon, as would be the Romans, or far above the Olympus, as would be the Greeks. This heaven is already inhabited by all the Jews, Catholics, Muslims and so many other fatalists, fanatics and radicals who abandoned the Tragic long ago in exchange for the certainty of salvation and for the ontological comfort of their new manger. Living became the art of waiting, patient, civilized, elegant, hygienic and Apollonian: in summation, being nothing more than a perfect cell of the body-state, half-way to heaven.

Those who believe themselves to be artists enlightened by the heavens, please, face this last proposition as no more than an aesthetic possibility. Only thus can we proceed with this challenge of ours. It is still worth recalling that, keeping it all in perspective, both Newton and Cervantes inspired themselves in life's peculiar but possible, that is, intelligible observations/sensations; such being the case, they may and must, when assuming the condition of metaphor or myth, go far beyond this given peculiarity.

So crazy is this life or existence, animated or not, that one its favorite traits are uncertainty and unpredictability. For those who still doubt, it suffices they witness their own annihilation. No matter how much we try to explain it or equate it, we cannot go much beyond the stillborn equations of logic, or the most inspired artistic endeavors, regardless of how many possibilities they might suggest or propose.

As much as we try to deny it, hiding behind elaborated metaphysics, Darwin's ideas[20] about natural selection may be expanded and, with a good infusion of poetic license, extended to every animated being that walks through time. The only thing that really assures permanence to things in this world, ideas included — artistic or scientific as they might be — is ultimately its capacity to adapt in the jungle of existence.

Randomness dominates existence in an inexorable way, and this frightens us terribly. We are condemned by our own discernment to live in a tight and dark tunnel; and the so called Will is the only weapon we possess to free our inconsequential child and convince it to escape the claws of superego and to go play outside, in places never visited before. Here I speak of matters of man, not of superman, therefore, outside is any space-time the still escapes our comprehension.

Seeing very little, for the light is still weak, we try to proceed, searching for an exit of which existence we are not certain at all, not to mention its unknown location. As prisoners in solitary confinement, we either die — which is not that easy — or start in-

---

20 Darwin, C. *On the Origin of Species*.

venting and elaborating all kinds of possibilities: metaphysical, physical, artistic and so on and so forth. Consciousness, the tyrant who holds us captive, is the same one that sets us free — an endless tyranny. When rising above all mortals, Icarus[21] lost control of his supreme freedom; and witnessed his own annihilation before the splendid Light. His stupendous audacity was punished harshly.

Madness and schizophrenia chase us incessantly, as tyrannical and macabre nightmares. At the slightest negligence, consciousness collapses in the abyss where things can no longer reach a possibility, not even a quantum or fractal one. We are condemned to clear other paths and to always establish possibilities.

I insist that such considerations are not metaphysical, though they might seem that way to the ill-advised who insist on getting some fake comfort by leaning on dogmas. Imminent disorder — demanded and imposed by the entropy that permeates everything — is anchored as a last resort against its return when solidified in the absolute geometry of a crystal. Thus, to affirm that the same spirit that animated primordial life also animates the birth of a Myth is a structural possibility, not a dogma.

---

21 Brandão, J. *Dicionário Mítico-Etimológico*.

Art animates Dialectics, which sustains a structure that branches beyond the limits of the sky. Mimesis seems to be the only path to self-understanding available to the flow of life. To generate possibilities, to create intelligible things or situations — "to let your brain reign" — is the price paid by the individual when allowing the Creator to experience the suffering of his Creature within Himself. Thus, we deny and affirm it is possible that Epistemology, Metaphysics and Art intersect in some time-location, perhaps on the borderline of the singularity of a black hole.

In the impossibility of questioning its present state — more anachronistic, inflexible, greasy and gigantic than ever, much like the last dinosaurs — Art advances tyrannically, maybe vengefully — as the worm whose only fate is to rot the apple — towards the temple of the highest order, the organized body of man, a cell in its ultimate state: Body Art! The analogical boundaries of the physical body can no longer be responsible for the virtual re-invention of space-time.

Ubiquity leaves the analogical imaginary behind to materialize in the virtual world. Its software enhance our senses, our memory. Frontiers crumble, crushed by the traffic and flux of all kinds of virtualities. Man mimics the Creator — Himself a human creation — to give meaning to a consciousness he already owns, prior to anything, with absolute power granted to Him by a lord whose only hope is to remain a penitent and a slave in his own right.

In the following lines, I will transubstantiate the sixth paragraph of the first topic, certain in this way to better expose Epistemology as Poetic Art:

> *"Myth is one of the most perfect and subtle manifestations of the Tragic, given that, more than any other manifestation, it embodies quite well conscious doing,* self-conscious, *and unconscious doing,* non-self-conscious, *the two elements of human action or the Action of Doing. These two parts of the action in each of us may be compared, or better still described as one, the part responsible for intelligibility and the other, for dealing with uncertainty, freedom and frankness. The necessary combination of them both in one or more Possibilities results of their necessary combination in human action."*

Even the Catholic church — that so elegantly and coherently embodies Platonism, a given metaphysical basis to Christianity — tries in the writings of Pope John Paul II[22]

---
[22] Pope John Paul II. *Letter to Artists*.

to conciliate the dogmatism of metaphysics with the Action of Doing, or the effort of man to interpret the unknown. Let us examine the words of His Holiness: "Every genuine artistic intuition goes beyond what the senses perceive and, reaching beneath reality's surface, strives to interpret its hidden mystery. The intuition itself springs from the depths of the human soul, where the desire to give meaning to one's own life is joined by the fleeting vision of beauty and of the mysterious unity of things."

About the Crisis of Utopias

Under the aegis of Christian aesthetics, the artists, or those who create, were suddenly seen as the new representatives and ambassadors of the Creator. They are "the chosen," the "illuminated," and some of them, even with no intellectual training, are capable of building unimaginable monuments before Him, as did Mozart, Einstein, Shakespeare, Galileo, Michael Jackson and Pelé.

All of the above, as we are aware, are regarded as geniuses and even saints. Little consideration is given to how much they might have fought and how many times they might have fallen, fed by the Tragic, in order to build their deeds. Time and necessity were responsible for making them immaculate, the possessors of a "divine gift." The subject-matter gets even more convoluted as the subject sees himself as "the One" and his sense of otherness is entirely lost; he forgets the paths to take in his preparation and starts behaving ultimately as one who is allowed to speak with the owner of Heaven and Earth. The Talent justifies the State. The Genius is the State itself, while the Tragic either dislocates the State in the direction of possible reforms, or ends up behind bars, gagged, under the guillotine.

Perhaps one of the most sophisticated utopias inspired by platonic Christianity, Marxism promised to bring Heaven to the Earth. Thus, it would be possible for every race to enjoy the same boon as King David and his children while still alive. Karl Marx's[23] aesthetic proposition was so endearing that more than half of the world, at some point in history, tried to build with his blessing a state of eternal happiness before his dream became a nightmare, the dictatorship of the proletariat.

In yet another illusion the Marxist state believed that it would be possible to demote the Tragic creators, from their condition of saints in the Christian utopia to that of edu-

---

23 Marx, K. *Capital*.

cators, ambassadors of the State itself. Things have not changed much. The problem is that the subject, worse than being demoted, has now to contend not only with the hereafter, but also with the Lord Himself — the State and its spokesmen, considering State as nothing but a metaphor of man materialized through a set of rules and laws, let us not forget, made by man himself as a convincing Mimesis of Social Man or a moral possibility for the Citizen: as is the case in Homer's *Odyssey*, where the hero Odysseus takes on the role of State. At the apogee of Marxism, everything seemed so ideally beautiful that it was almost forbidden not to be an artist or a citizen involved in its ideals.

According to my belief, not even Marx himself was so seriously attached to his own aesthetic proposition of the State; as a matter of fact, Marx was never a Marxist, only a novelist that was taken literally. Everything was but an attempt to overcome two great examples of Tragic subjects, one of them the undeniable Homer, who outlined Greek culture with the *Iliad* and the *Odyssey*. Through his lyricism, in a single stroke Homer reinvented man, sky, Earth and, what is more interesting, the ambiguous as a possibility. The other is Plato, an antithesis to Homer who established the basis for the Dialectic and, as a consequence, for Logic. While elevating rhetoric to the universe of Logic, Plato was the founder of modern philosophy.

It is worth noting that Marx, even after the fall of most Marxist states, is still revered for his accomplishments and marches steadily towards his canonization by the Vatican, even if this Vatican is in Africa, in the mountains of Latin America, etc. Wisely, Christian churches of all denominations tried to reconcile those two utopias, what appears to be slowing down its final demise — better still, giving them profit — resulting in the surge of a new aesthetic called Social Inclusion. Or would the later be a new utopia, towards which all the others are converging, hoping to expiate, in a single act, all of man's evil in this age of information? [As far as I'm concerned, I neither oppose nor favor this proposition, since I haven't formed an opinion.]

What scares us today is the unspoken obligation of taking Social Inclusion into consideration with every undertaking, whatever the project, especially if it involves the State. What is very romantic is that it has reached the sphere of elegance and has ended up becoming currency, especially to those most skilled in the dealings of government and corporations. It is just as hard to deny its importance as to predict the consequences of this willful inclusion at any price: "God does not help those who do not help themselves." It is easy to testify to the appearance of a new tribe of pariahs who do not fit in any inclusionary group. And how can we work this out, when we face the risk of seeing the return of the old slogan for the collapse of Marxism, now modified: "I pretend to include you and you pretend you are being included."

In this new aesthetic, the Tragic is replaced by piety and compassion. Social Inclusion is a parameter for everything, from classroom work to grand social events. The courage and the healthy transgression expressed by the "tragic ones" now result in sin, that leads to Hell, invented by Dante the Christian[24] and based on Homer's *Odyssey*. The hero Odysseus[25] goes as far as exchanging ideas with the inhabitants of Hades, a sketch of Hell that inspired so many with its unparalleled plasticity. We find ourselves on a dead-end road.

In this scenario, what is truly perplexing is the fact that the practice of Social Inclusion promotes a kind of self-indulgence, a guarantee of Heaven for the penitent. It gets worse when you realize that "Inclusion" may grow in direct proportion to the sinner's assets. How to avoid falling into this trap, pleasing

---

24 Alighieri, D. *A Divina Comédia*.
25 Homero. *Odisseia*. (Trans. by Donaldo Schuler, 2007)..

to the Majority, especially to social leaders filled with guilt? According to Voltaire's Candide,[26] a favorite of all who believe in utopia as a means, no matter what diverse interests they might have, "a better world is possible."

I do not know if a world that is better or worse is possible. What I do know is that composing possibilities is our yoke, even a matter of survival. The great playwright Bertolt Brecht[27] claims, with much propriety: "*There are men who struggle for a day and they are good. There are men who struggle for a year and they are better. There are men who struggle many years, and they are better still. But there are those who struggle all their lives: These are the indispensable ones,*" a widely disseminated quote, but still worthy of mentioning, thought-provoking to the point of justifying utopias. Many insist, and have insisted, in classifying Brecht as a Marxist. It may well be true. But he was, above all, an unparalleled Tragic conductor, waving his baton at the score he mythicized through his plays.

Would not "Social Inclusion" be the Capitalist Utopia's antidote for its own imminent death? I would simply ask: how to be Tragic and at the same time keep practicing

---

26 Voltaire. *Candide*.
27 Brecht, B. *Plays, Poetry and Prose*.

Inclusion, as most people do? I believe myself to be on my way to Hell, as a Catechism teacher once told me. As a *mea culpa*, I propose an Intellectual Inclusion crusade for everyone, including *intellectual dilettantes*. Would I not be one of them myself? I claim not, but as Pirandello[28] observed: "Things are not as they are, but as they seem to be."

Just as Christianity, Islam, a doctrine of salvation, promises to its more than faithful, "predestined" followers the Heaven of David. With the permission of all, I claim that Muslims, "the ones who submit," are the first reformed Christians. Let us not forget that the sons of Islam accept both Moses with his book the Torah, and Jesus with the Gospels. They see Christ as just another prophet who preceded Mohammed, the world's ultimate enlightened soul.

The certainty of a Heaven with Virgins, as everything else in the Islamic world, gives way to an almost complete elimination of Tragic behavior. It is easy to observe that for them an existential dialectic is as inexistent as the basic question that puzzles most of the Western world: "Where have we come from and where do we go next?" Their art has no more than a theological purpose. Theater poses no questions. Everything seems to be

---

28 Pirandello, L. *Right You Are, If You Think You Are.*

explained by the Quran: too bad the character from the First Soliloquy, previously described, does not know it. What matters is to live obediently waiting for the stately Heavens.

It is interesting to observe that, while the Greek would not avoid Hades, a tenebrous and sinister place, the Christian may travel almost freely between Heaven and Hell as Dante did. Mohammed would give it full measure with his rules and prayers, promising Heaven to all believers; it does not take much alms, or penitence or Social Inclusion. It is enough to fulfill some minor promises — such as, for instance, to bring down the Twin Towers, the greatest symbol of capitalism — and everything will be settled forever, at least in the minds of most Shiites. One could say that, since Marx was not a Marxist, Mohammed was nothing but a sociologist whose doctrine was adopted, most of the time inappropriately, by several nation-states, especially in the Arab world.

Art is the enemy of certainty. Its expression should be ambiguous and doubtful, as well as questioning, never at the service of any ideology or utopia, whether metaphysical, sociological or any other. Antigone should be Art's name. The Tragic, that in its own way moves people and states, is made of tradition, will, courage and desire; it feeds the creator, the desperate and the neurotic who end up making its metaphysics their own art or expression, their utopia.

The days of Engaged Art and creation in the service of utopias and all else are numbered. The nourishment of Art should be non-conformism, the non-acceptance of any reality as final. The freedom in exercising the Tragic is the only possibility of a man following Socrates' guiding rule to "know thyself," later in time bastardized by the Christians as their own beautiful and dangerous "Love thy neighbor as thyself" and by the Muslims as their not less beautiful and sophisticated "Acquire knowledge: it makes its possessor able to distinguish right from wrong," an aphorism that might well explain Islamic growth nowadays. With the help of excerpts from the book *Vianinha*, by Fernando Peixoto,[29] I created a hypothetical dialogue between two Brazilian playwrights, Vianninha and Nelson Rodrigues, that might help illustrate the crisis of utopias herein discussed. Vianninha is spelled with two N's in the dialogue below and with one in the title of the book, and I followed suit.

---

29 Peixoto, F. *Vianinha: Teatro, Televisão, Política*.

Dialogue: "Reactionary vs Marxist"

Vianninha: *I think as a writer you're very sincere, never putting down on paper what is demanded by social pressure, writing whatever goes through your head. You are what you write and, maybe because of that, a good artist. Nelson, only D. Jaime Câmara could deny the artist in you; and therefore, of course, your quite fair indignation for being labeled a reactionary. A "right-wing" man, according to you, knows he is a "right-winger" and boasts about it; he is nauseated when he sees a worker, lights up a vigil candle for Rockefeller, does not watch your plays, knows nothing about* candomblé, *has never heard of Garrincha, wears a cassock at home.*

Nelson: *For an old man like myself, a mummy really, it is delicious to debate with the new generations. However, my chat with Vianninha has a technical flaw. I ask, how to argue with someone I call by a pet name? Yes,* *how do I curse someone whom I call, laughingly, "Vianninha"?*

Vianninha: *You are inflexible, Nelson; no beating around the bush. That's where the stamina and violence in your plays come from; your dialogue is rough, dry, without any buts or trinkets — your words are mismatched, they don't fit exactly into a logical and quiet order. Your dialogue, damn good, is as intransigent as you are. You don't give the* petit bourgeois *a break, always bundling your aspirations and wills together to alienate yourself from "this way is better," or "here we can handle it." You don't want order, you want passion pure and clear, as if you didn't need an ideological ground in order to exist, to make yourself manifest.*

Nelson: *Why does my Cuban colleague bitch about me? I say Cuban and I explain it: Vianninha lives physically in Brazil; but his sentimental and ideological residence is in Cuba. His process of alienation might make him even more confused — I will someday see*

Vianninha consulting a tourist map to discover where Downtown Rio is.

Vianninha: *I think, Nelson, that society formed a new man, a social man like there has never been before, connected to another in order to survive, to be fed, to have fun, and everything else. Social consciousness has to accept this for a fact, adapt to it, master it and move forward; in their minds: each man for himself and not even God to give him a hand. And this contradiction is getting more and more violent. Man loses his humanity; the awareness of his necessities is lost. He needs to think really hard in order to re-conquer himself, and you are scribbling over the thought process. You are a reactionary, Nelson Rodrigues.*

Nelson: *In his deepest resentment, Vianninha denies my theater from top to bottom. And why is that? It is simple: because I'm not involved in political propaganda, because I don't swallow sectarian art. In short, Vianninha wanted "The Golden Mouth" to stop the* *play and introduce a statement of ideology. And more, he's not satisfied with the characters, he also demands the same from the playwright himself. I wish to ask Vianninha: "Hey boy!!! Are you a revolutionary or a cop?"*

Vianninha: *Your limited vision of the* petit bourgeoisie *such as ourselves generalizes inappropriately. Your plays never leave the bedroom at all. Their geographic location is always at places of consumption, never of production. Your plays praise the individual who gave up his highest will to get a grip on reality and decided to spend the rest of his life effulgently, stumbling, screaming and beating his own chest like an animal, happy for not having to think: The exaltation of the marginalization, exaltation and cheers to the man who left his humanness behind.*

Nelson: *Good old Engels, the grandfather of today's Marxists, in a letter written to Minna Kautsky said, "I am far from finding fault with you for not having written a point-blank socialist novel, a 'Tendenzroman' as we Ger-*

mans call it, to glorify the social and political views of the author." [That is not at all what I, Nelson, mean.] "The more the opinions of the author remain hidden, the better for the work of art. The realism I am referring to is manifested independently from the author's opinions."

Vianninha: *What's all that, Nelson? You are being left behind — that's why you covered me with feathers. I am not a chickenshit Marxist, I am not a wren or a hummingbird. Your sincerity is starting to wear off. More and more, you want to be seen as a good author; more and more an author in other people's opinion.*

Nelson: *Don't get desperate, Vianninha, take a look: Engels himself professed, with the most brutal nonchalance, to prefer Balzac over all present, past and future Zolas. In the preface to the* Comédie Humaine, *Engels threw this bomb,* "J'écris à la lueur de deux vérités éternelles, la religion et la monarchie." *Marx also used to put Balzac up in Heaven. Vian-*

ninha, Marx himself! I repeat, good old Marx was an utmost bewildered and clerical monarchist!

Vianninha: *Nelson, you are being defensive, what explains your attack on chickens and Engels. It's good to put up a fight. A good plan. But you started off on the wrong foot, clinging to your subject of choice, profiting from past applause. You are playing around with old accomplishments in spite of future ones, lecturing people with a dossier under your arm, wandering about as man of the cloth, a plantation master or a corrupt politician.*

Nelson: *Check how relentless the dialogue between two generations can be! Vianninha and I speak the same idiom, I mean, I speak Brazilian and Vianninha speaks Cuban. But it is not language that keeps us apart — we could find ourselves an interpreter. What keeps us apart is age. We are two different epochs in a spitting contest.*

Vianninha: *Your characters never have*

a rational or consciousness problem, where their actions submit to an agenda, to reasons and motifs seen from the perspective of man's conditioning. It is always about unleashed passions that need to clash against the given order to be fulfilled. But this order is the usual and forever discussed story. All your characters, in their thinking, degrade themselves.

In May of 1975, according to Fernando Peixoto, Nelson Rodrigues would affirm to *Jornal do Brasil* that "Rend Your Heart," the play by Oduvaldo Viana Filho (Vianinha), at that time censored by the Dictatorship, was "one of the most beautiful and fascinating masterpieces in Brazilian theater." In 1979, on the opening night, Nelson testified again: "The great play by Vianna, 'Rend Your Heart' has an impressive, very exciting Dionysian tension." Only recently Rodrigues has been granted his deserved position among those we can call the Tragic Ones.

About the Post-Crisis of Utopias

To begin this topic, let me describe a soliloquy about de-globalization that will reinforce the workings of this essay. Fill your lungs with air and please, read without punctuation, without stopping. Forget prosody. Proceed like a car careening downhill with no brakes. Let loose all restraints from the *self-conscious* and the *non-self-conscious*, and to what purpose? It is perhaps the mere influence of self-help literature, what can be done about it? Let's! One... two... three... go!

The Second Soliloquy: "A Fragment of de-globalization"

"He has half the deed done who has made

a beginning," a dried-out and still valid quote from Plato — who, by being envious of Heraclitus, invented the lyricism of pure reason, founded the world of imaging, invented the possibility of all that is possible. Inconsequent and lyrical, Heraclitus took human dimensions beyond the frontiers of Hades, surpassing the endless source of Possibilities... Possibilities of worlds of images, colors, dreams, all Heraclitus wanted was the eye of Tiresias; behind the blindness, a world beyond Plato... gods, humans and semi-gods sailing the same ship... Jealous, Plato designed the new world of the supremacy of the pure idea, *of unlimited reason, of the possible equation... a successful Pythagorean!! The* image-idea *achieves supremacy, history, the eternity of the belief in the* possible/ *reason... Christianities, Marxisms, Antropophagisms, Concretisms, they all thank Plato!! But bow before Heraclitian non-reason, owner of the "forthcoming math," lady of stochastic functions of the nth degree... unsolvable differential equations...Plato exists!! Exists and exist he will... for the Platonic, who from eternity contemplate the* fog/ smoke *that hovers over the* eternity/ abyss, *the image that's not the Word... That's not DO or REDO or UNDO... the world of the* CONTEMPLATION LOVERS/ IMAGEPHILIACS, *the eternal and fertile space for the infertility of voyeurs... They can't tell the deed from the land... the smoke from the flame... the sigh from the dream.... Only distance keeps them* INTACT, UNTOUCHABLE, SMOKEFOGBEINGS *in a* DISTANT, SAINTLY, PURE, IMACCULATE *gaze...* LONG LIFE TO ACRYLICS! *Kept safe by the Christian duality that always points out to* CLEANLINESS, *the* RECTITUDE OF THE SOUL *that saves itself, given that it's not involved... does not rebel... Static, at most, exercises contemplation... No practice, no strength, no will...only the letting go, invaded by a strange regard... How good it is that the world exists! May existence remain there! May it happen there...even if it does not...* SHOO, SHOO! DO, UNDO, REDOO, *as Bourgeois used to say, dancing in Bahia on Mardi Gras, even knowing that HOMER is the father of the pagan Bible, un-confessed CATECHESIS of all of humanity's great authors — epic or non-epic. Platonic Christianity in Greece, founded and anticipated Christianity itself. Theater, Greek arts and all the movements of that era bow before absolute Platonic order — thus is born the first virtual man: Plato. Before the Platonic depths, when everything seemed translated, understood, even Heraclitus lost his mystery. Euripides, his prodigal son and the first Christian of all, expelled the PAGAN gods from his stage... his stage of ideas... Ideas of Platonic INQUISITION, imagetic, equationable, entirely possible, a man with no mysteries... the STATE-MAN, the LOGIC-MAN... the SMOKE OF KARL MARX'S FIRST DREAMS; we stand before the first great DE-GLOBALIZATION... Greek hegemony dissolves before the weakness and frailty of Platonic Man, who at that given moment was stamped onto the ultimate sculpture of the Classic Period, with Phidias and all the others... THE TACTIC, THE HAPTIC AND THE OLFACTORY were buried deep with Tiresias, the only one who could see... the image acquired absolute divinity. The time had arrived for the* CONTEMPLATIVE/ IM-AGEPHILIACS, *TEMPLARIANS WITH NO SWORD!! And why not say it, WITHOUT A SCABARD? How crass is that, uh?? May the imagephiliacs forgive me, but that's what came up... the* OUTDOOR *Generation... the Media Generation... the Generation of profuse colors... the ultimate meal for those who favor retirement over ACTION... but order prevails, amoebas exist!! Phagocytes, phagocytize, phagocytized... Far ahead of Darwin, creatures generating creatures generating creatures, the absolute order of the lowest creatures... so small are they, that some descended directly from Lygia Clark's "creatures" and fell into the hands of the unaware, weird beings of order, disordered, misunderstood... at last, Man! This non-mysterious mystery prefers contemplation, another marble stone who gained shape — Classical, sometimes not so Classical, Modernist, sometimes POP... sometimes Concretist and even Dadaist... Con-*

structivism prevails!! Struggling against the unshakeable quantum of the minuscule, majuscule bowels of the Universe... it is the discreet/ non-continuous man searching Platonism in continuity... a unique place, a unique function, capable of existing in a need for order... the disorder, the chaos, the quantum... THEY ARE ALL OFFENSIVE! They bother, they sadden, they abandon Platonic guts and MAKE CLAIM for Heraclitus's irresponsibility... What to do about it? Order, disorder or singularity? I'm so glad we can still be Hamlets — thank you, Shakespeare... I look around, I type this text, I touch my mouse... and I touch the world... Order prevails!! Plato, THE ONLY NON-PLATONIC ONE... ends up being RIGHT! For being the only one who is ignorant of Heraclitus's non-reason, or his stupid/ singular reason, unqualified, threatening... what a great evil Darwin has done to us... He took Plato to his last consequences... only the fittest will survive, where are the dinosaurs and so many other creatures that this endless order condemned to extermination??

Where is Surrealism, and all the madness of unknown human pseudo-probings?? Another dinosaur grows, new beings now, beyond the Word/ flesh, they gain a voice... a life!! They start to con-judge-gate the verb virtualize... corporations swallow us... they turn us into cells, cells and more cells, that phagocytize in the guts of each unit of these beings that expand infinitely. Survival is the ultimate order of a PAGAN GOD. To grow is to survive... these new dinosaurs are thus created, in the laboratories of the Science Academies, now social, economic... The biological being is nothing but one cell of this grand creature that devours at any cost the forest of human pleasures, human curiosity, CREdulous, CREatable human... like cancer cells, making insane the members and pieces of these huge beings designed for absolute order. They grow towards the absolute, demolishing the great dinosaurs of our time... drowned in huge ciphers of virtual dollars... they tumbled, they fogged, they smoked this world, spreading dust to the most faraway corners of the planet. The Eski-

mo Sun finds the sky painted red... the polar bear shakes... but from heat... anguished, in the non-Euclidean geometry of a densely populated land. Art, that sees itself as Art as it stops being Art, expresses in its own construction the ultimate deconstruction of Derrida... The depth is not of interest anymore. Immediacy is the easy meal for all hours... training only motivates dogs, that cheer up the hospitals now void of children... May Uganda and Kenya be there for us, children of the world! Would not that be the fall of the virtuosi? Or the beginning of a new beginning? When simply abandoned, a risk, better yet, THE RISK, is the most plastic of all Contemporary Art — that is not on the wall, or in the man!! Only in a fragment of Duchampian waste that isn't Duchamp at all, translating the imminent dis-flavoring of the order, grounded in order itself, that steps on Tiresias, blind to the exterior world... Art, still claiming a function, even one of a second degree stochastic differential, can no more find its place... the real as the usurper of the virtual!! A virtual that is now real, what a sight, this Deleuzian horizon, abode to the new Christians who believe themselves to be re-drawing the New Art, the ultimate work, A FEAST ON THE SIDEWALK, or if you like, THE DOMESTIC EXPANDED. That's what I call "pursuing the ordinary guys" — a feast on the sidewalk. Now what is that, my friends from Minas and Pernambuco?? I'm glad that Duchamp has saved us, for everything now is Art!! Too bad some have taken Duchamp so seriously — a successful cartoonist, never more than that, I repeat and will repeat always, whether you like it or not: a great chess player in the land of Napoleon, or as could possibly be, a great performer/ comedian in New York and, I never understood exactly why, in Buenos Aires as well... iIf the new dinosaurs/ corporations have blown art up, is this what we're left with? Or the not-this? Whatever, and I'm glad it is so; we have discovered a wonderful thing, our greatest expression as the artists we now are, who pervade us. We are now the artists of ourselves, even as we sleep... imagine that... as you or I walk around, imbued with action/ non-action/ randomness, *we create a big masterpiece, unparalleled, inimitable!! Funny enough, I feel we just accomplished the understanding of Contemporary Art: suffice it to be, why bother to become, no? One plus one equal more or less two, and don't be scared, we are talking about the quantum where we search for possibilities, weak as they might be, yet the ultimate expression of man's inexactitude: a stinking smelling listening creature who touches and eats, or dis-eats, and strange as it may be, self-multiplies having order as a given... the order... the eternal order... intrigues. How to disclose the possibility of impossibilities in the Odyssean world that scared Plato and the penicillin world so badly? The hecatomb is here, the De-globalization invades our frontiers, non-interfacing: My Territory, Your Territory, our territories shrink in an unprecedented disorder, searching for further disorder amidst such lack of order... such disorder, nevertheless, maintains the new creature still hidden, restricted, lacerated, although starting its appearance in the middle of total and urgent disorder... thanks to you, Darwin, we can be the occasional mammal... And if it's not so, who cares, so many have tried, and then, what? Natural Selection be damned, the anti-species can speak louder than that... mistaken or not, our own creature wants more space, to escape verticality... a creature is born on the skyline... branching is for everyone else... The creature intends to INHABIT THE PLAINS, at most the plateau, where LACANIAN CREATIVISM reigns! It is the TRAGIC-ART creature... the NEOMAMMAL! Thus is born the HOMOTRAGICUS!!.*

Do not reread what you just read. Whatever your feelings, reader dear, save them to feed what is still left to read, that is, if I have not lost you. All is well! It's time to move on. While utopias and their possibilities wear down and fall apart, two opposing kinds of survivors appear as a possible foundation for a world that now re-grounds: the domesticated, who flow into the galleries, stages and streets displaying redundancies stolen from a past Myth that haunts and weakens; and a minority of fanatics open to anything, willing to go to extremes with their beliefs in utopias already fallen, or still moribund.

Most of the time, the proposed solution ends up corroborating life's hidden desires compelled to defy any programming or utopia, whether Existentialist, Capitalist, Marxist or even Metaphysical. What reminds me of Erasmus of Rotterdam, in *The Praise of Folly*:

"But 'tis a sad thing, they say, to be mistaken. Nay rather, he is most miserable that is not so."

"For so great is the obscurity and variety of human affairs that nothing can be clearly known."

And still: "…men so bewitched with this present hope that it never repents them of their pains or expense, but are ever contriving how they may cheat themselves."

Art — in fact, epistemology and utopia — is nothing but a subterfuge we create to anchor our own loneliness and the extreme meaninglessness of existence. By saying these words I am led, as an exile from my own self, to the feelings and agonizing sensations of being crucified in a storm. Take this empty *chalice away from my Self*! As Solomon says in the Book of Ecclesiastes, "*everything is futility and striving after wind.*" "All our heroes died from overdosing," howled Cazuza, the Brazilian poet, in his Tragic and suicidal life's trajectory.

All we are left with is the renewed exercise of the Tragic. It seems to be our only way-out. If annihilation is inevitable, let's make it our ally. May the world be filled with Quixotes, Aristotles, Dylans, Jaggers, Riobaldos and Odyssei. Let's not spare our courage. And may Heaven go, with or without virgins, to fanatics and Shias. To make Art, Art and Poetic Epistemology, that's what is left to us. Engaged Art is jobless. Art, sedentary and *replicant*, is at the service of a moribund and tottering Capitalism.

The last strongholds that still deny the world of things are about to explode; thus I hope! The days of Art and Professional Artists are numbered; thus I hope! Creating or proposing possibilities is our Darwinist destiny — to proceed with the logical order that allows us to exist and know it; thus I hope! Social Inclusion will only come through by way of the Tragic and the Knowing; thus I hope! The Tragic ones will dig deep, much beyond the continuous, the fractal, the quantum and the singularity, searching for the ultimate fate, however mobile, of the *black hole,* its distempers and discernments never imagined in our Kingdom of Will, forever DO, UNDO and REDO;[30] thus I hope!

To the modern ones in all times, I urge

---

30 Bourgeois, L. *TATE*.

them to carefully consider their uncontrollable will to deny everything, especially their tragic condition: the only human element capable of initiating, promoting a revision and displacement of the world. The imposition, the persecution of an art based on the denial of possibilities — complete and even stochastic, or quantum, or as some academics prefer, devoid of outlines or blueprints — is nothing but another deficient and inexpressive kind of decision or possibility, the true owners of "weirdo art." I am grateful for their existence: for only thus can we know for sure what not to do. The great problem is the distance, so far and so close, between the Modern, alias, the Eternal, and the Modernoid. How vast can our vain philosophy, or better yet, our utmost folly be?

I would like to allow myself a prayer, recited by Medea in a personal adaptation of the Euripides's play I've been trying for years to put on. It contains and metaphorizes all my feelings about the world and Post-Utopian Art. The best way to be a pagan, I believe, is to dress yourself as a Christian and pray a mass to Dionysus. I was just reminded of the great Portuguese poet Fernando Pessoa's desire to be a pure Greek pagan, when embodying his heteronym Alberto Caeiro, the anti-philosopher who composed "The

Keeper of Herds."[31] The more Caeiro denies metaphysics and philosophy, the more his Christianity becomes clear. Good! Fernando Pessoa, at least, acknowledged the weight of Christianity in his literature.

Prayer: "The myth of Each Day or a Pagan Prayer"

Contemporary heroes... plastic fleece... rudderless ship... my holy Joan of Arc... latest sacrifice... contradiction that art on earth... our Tragic that is in heaven... great and frightening be thy name... thy spirit of courage come... the ultimate hero of the Calvary mount... Possibilities be done... on earth as it is in heaven... give us this day our daily Myth... activate us and our desires... as we activate those whom we desire... and lead us not into too-many-actions, but deliver us from the sedentary, the penitent art, the mommy's artist, from the self-help enlightened, the utilitarian art... and from ourselves… Amor!

---

31 Pessoa, F. *Poética II, poemas de Alberto Caeiro.*

Being suggestible and suggesting: that is the tension that governs the Tragic and all its configurations, unintelligible as they may seem. Will and desire, the intrigues of many philosophers, are the only eyes capable of realizing a possibility still lost in the heart of Logos. Dealing with the mystery of the unknown brings Art and Metaphysics together, but they both should question why epistemology influences art and even Metaphysics, while it should be and has always been the other way around... the deed turned back upon the doer. Dionysus and Apollo observe each other in a rhythmic and frenetic dance. The persistent art of the illuminated and the self-hallowed is mixed-up with a metaphysics that hides beneath the blind fanaticism of idiots. Spinozan[32] longitudes and latitudes support and imbricate the *self-conscious* and the *non-self-conscious* doings.

Art and the contemporary world are, both, literally lost. Utopias of every order fed the construction of States that, although bankrupt, will take years to dissolve, and in the vortex of their fall, the heinous Engaged and Opportunistic Art will disappear. Art, as a herald of the ethical, the aesthetic and moral freedom of expression still walks a narrow path, between the tyranny of a moralistic,

---

32 Deleuze, G. *Spinoza: Practical Philosophy.*

decadent State, and a herd of scared individuals charging an ever-growing price for civility and the lobotomy of artistic expression. The thing is to maintain their comfort and the Establishment at all costs, for they have a mortgage to pay. It makes me wonder if the evil eye that keeps "bread and circuses" art alive will prevail.

Let us move on to another soliloquy, this time, a dramatized critique, or something like it, of the process of University education that is dominant in these days of mandatory Social Inclusion. All I do is criticize, for it is so easy to do so. And don't ask me for a solution that I don't have: how difficult can it be for the University to graduate students that can be critical? By valuing historical, instead of critical knowledge, the World Wide Web of information — the Internet — appears as an answer, a ubiquitous memory, doubtlessly a virtual extension of our still analogical brain, nothing a mouse will not solve. I believe we are facing a new Utopia, Metaphysics dissolved in Pythagorean digits.

Third soliloquy: "The 'fast-food' university and the 'delivery' student"

Time in these times accrues more and

more sovereign-pride, an unlimited contempt for an ever weirder conception of space. What is this space? We can no longer remember, or what it is used for. We are submerged in virtuality... cine-photos... momenta-photos and so many other photos spread along an endless horizon: without any temporal sequence at all, they invade our being with a worn-out ontology. The world freezes in juxtaposed images, imposed over its existence, time throbs, pulsates, loses its own verticality and sprawls on this horizon of photos — the virtual willing to become real... But unguided time pulsates... moving time in all possible directions... pushing the Doings, the Deeds and the To-Dos towards a non-temporal blackening hole, *the singularity, the last moment of Myth, that still does not know if born materially or nightmarized... to impose insatiable needs, the Tragic of Sublime Will... the thirst in the dry-arid-desert... to impose ambition and take us all to the farthest limit. Who the hell wants to lose this race whose secret only time knows, no one, nothing — time, the absolute Lord of*

Slavespace *that now falls, submissive, on his knees, perhaps for having played a role in the world of dialectical thinking. After Lacan, we have tried living Art in quantum unconsciousness, but time flies in commanding speed that being extreme takes time to disordered madness, so everything and everyone can run even further: it is the* FAST-FOOD ERA. *Formal teaching abandons content, as it follows success at all costs… the success of a McDonald's package* photoshape, *that with insatiable hunger becomes whole at the speed of delivery, for these times now being… in the fury of not losing their race, the runners are whorified, drug-addicted to form and volume… The more the better — the law of survival, where stronger is faster and only winning matters — don't stay behind, don't be forgotten in time. People pack,* secularize *— sliced students, simple and tasty, burgerized, BigMacsized satisfying their* photomedia, photoflavored *demands… everything dead or delivered in a photovirtual reality still trying to become Art in its ultimate desire to betray its own software,* *or black box... as spatial* quanta, *configured by an erring gaze, trained in the Eternal Return. This is a picture... this is another picture, that's how pictures are... said our very dear and only Brazilian philosopher, Vilém Flusser. The Information Age! Someone thus baptized this tempest point in which we live,* virtualive. *Can we still, after the* Big Mac crash *of the Dot-com Bubble, call it that? Whose bang bubbled waves and tides and even tiny ripples, in fact checkbook ledgers, shocking even sovereign time? Leave divination to the oracles, it is too soon, we're immersed in unknown waves, and what good is that? What we live through is the manufacturing, the packaging, the shipping and handling of* fast-food-students, *it's too bad they forgot, that they never learned from Mr. McDonald how to put themselves in a* photoknowledge, *better still, a* photosmell. *Therefore, they would go unnoticed by the nuances of the markets with no logo, no owner, with no other wish but overcoming time. The unprecedented competition of teaching institutions, in order to better and faster deliver its* package-students, *allied to this constant, disorderly world crisis, have created a new, and mostly feared, specimen of* educator — *the* McDonald cook, *or the one who survived the downsizing of the board of teachers of these schools, insane about being on top, their only concern in these limitless times. The primary imprint of this* educator, *master, doctor, or post-doctor, what kept him in these institutions, is knowing, as nobody terraqueous else, how to nullify all his wants and desires, giving absolute priority to the only thing he really knows, and has always known: TO FULFILL HIS DUTY, HIS OBLIGATION to copy well the established and standardized knowledge, with no afterthoughts or doubting, and thus,* Christian-like, *being worthy of the Kingdom of Heaven, his meager and doleful pay — a pile of* impaired-photos, *backed by* hero-symbols, *bygone and decadent, just another* vapid-photo. *All of this in a* vigilantmanagingsoftware, *so that, as in the many McDonalds of this life, a replication of the number of* delivery-students *will be possible ad infinitum.*

What matters is that the students are delivered on time, just like everyone else who will never mutate or adapt to other levels — equally virtualized *and annihilated, unsuitable for the generation of species and differences, for the survival and continuity of the ontological and knowing. It is forbidden to desire. In order to maintain these factories of* replicants*, everything is permitted. We stand before a* student-subject, *a photocopy of all the standards in use by each* school-educator, *the cruel reality of coming advisors who now abandon their position as dialectical animators. It is forbidden to think. I think, therefore I am not. Thus is born the new Judas, the "Judas of the Information Age," who thinks, and worse than that, who speaks and asks — we thank you, René Descartes, a reborn Greek who escaped the bonfire thanks to the loneliness of his preaching. A renovated* educator-consulting, *winged and alien, seems to be coming from the guts of this smooth and deserted world of* xeroxed replicants *in the age of information. It is the* creature-website *of the* webian *world... it does not matter, now I know, I am nothing in this world but a lonely neuron in a huge brain, what can be done about it? At least, this* endless-creature *still considers me, even in my most extreme need. With my infinite* mouseated *finger, I touch in excitement, sexually even, parts of this newborn being, taking form, in fact, taking time. How to understand that? On one side of the* wall-time, *more and more* fast-foodian, deliverian *students, trained to love the certainty of copying and to deny the doubting and uncertainty of the dialectic; on the other,* neuronbeings *that, in this* webian *world, unprecedentedly capture everyone and everything... WIKIPEDIA! That puts to shame and depression the wisest of* memories-educators, *and now they all know, they remember it all, in any language... REPLICATED-REPLICANT-TEACHERS, and now what? A memory in seconds, a memory for what? Where is my* educactor, *my* cogito-professor? *"Cogito, ergo sum," or better still: I CLICK, THEREFORE I AM.*

With these last sayings, I reaffirm my belief in the possibility of placing the study and practice of Art into the field of epistemology, forever abandoning the search and canonization of talents and geniuses, almost always hidden behind some coward and fearsome training. Art and creation are inalienable rights of each of us. Composing and precipitating Myths, ambiguous as they can possibly be, is a need of the Tragic in us, which can only be full if freed from obligations of any kind. Reinventing the wheel is a task for the intellectually excluded; everything else is a Duchampian jocosity taken seriously by some. The only way out is the *pythagorization* of the world, not forgetting the *non-self-consciousness*. In his Tragic obsession, Pythagoras claimed that someday everything will be resolved in numbers, and ended up by bravely writing the music and the sound: Logos became Word and Word became Musical Score.

There must be, for discernment's sake, a moment and place, even utopian, where total ambiguity reigns, where Possibilities may differentiate as stem-cells in every order/ organ, from the most subtle and suggestive ones, as in expressions of art —including the stupid ones, often the most Tragic and strange — to the most platonic, like the Alpha station that orbits out there in the confines of the skies as a flying pyramid, inviting us to travel beyond the little art and limited creation that surround us due to the abandonment of the Tragic.

The decadence of this creature-man is nothing but the translation of our complete apathy towards this world, in the certainty of the Other created by ourselves, capable of atonement for all our evils, fears and solitude. We have to recover, at all costs, our fears and uncertainties, in order to take them even deeper in our anguish and explore, as lucid lunatics, every detail of what's unknown beyond the singularity. If need be, let us pierce our own eyes as Oedipus did, in order to look beyond the curtain of logic and enigmas.

Our only light must be lit with the torch of epistemological lucidity. There will not be space for the Illuminated and the Guessing Charlatans who dominate the lying academies of our time. Art for art's sake, as our last and ultimate utopia, is the crusade we propose. There will not be space for metaphysics of any order. The Tragic that tensions and drives us is a temple of Possibilities that is neither means nor end: it is a dialectic or even a non-dialectic flow of facts and courage.

I have spoken!

About the Bibliographic References

Alighieri, D. *A Divina Comédia*. Porto Alegre: L&PM, 2006.

Aristóteles. *Poética*. (Portuguese translation by J. Bruna). São Paulo: Cultrix, 1981.

Bourgeois, L. *TATE*. Londres: Tate Modern Gallery, 2000.

Brandão, J. *Dicionário Mítico-etimológico*. Rio de Janeiro: Vozes, 1991.

Brecht, B. *Poesia, Textos, Teatro*. Lisboa: Dinossauro, 1998.

Brecht, B. *Teatro Dialético*. São Paulo: Civilização Brasileira, 1967.

Costa, L. M. A *Poética de Aristóteles — Mimese/ Verossimilhança*. São Paulo: Ática, 1992.

Darwin, C. *A origem das espécies*. São Paulo: Escala, 2008.

Davis, M. *The Poetry of Philosophy On Aristotle's Poetics*. South Bend, Indiana: St Augustine's Press, 1992.

Deleuze, G. *Espinosa, Filosofia Prática*. São Paulo: Escuta, 2002.

Descartes, R. *Discurso do Método*. Porto Alegre: L&PM, 2007.

Grassi, E. *Arte como antiarte*. São Paulo: Duas cidades, 1975.

Homero. *Odisseia*. (Portuguese Translation by D. Schuler). Porto Alegre: L&PM, 2007.

Houaiss, A. *Dicionário Eletrônico — Assinantes UOL*. São Paulo, 2009.

Lima, L. *O Controle do Imaginário*. São Paulo: Brasiliense, 1984.

Marx, K. *Capital*. London: Lawrence & Wishart, 1970.

Melquior, J. *A Astúcia da Mimese*. Rio de Janeiro: José Olímpio, 1972.

Newton, I. *Principia*. São Paulo: Edusp Nova Stella, 1990.

Nietzsche, F. *Assim Falou Zaratustra*. Rio de Janeiro: Bertrand, 1995.

Paulo II, João. *Carta do Papa aos Artistas*. São Paulo: Paulinas, 2003.

Peixoto, F. *Vianinha: Teatro, Televisão, Política*. São Paulo: Brasiliense, 1983.

Pessoa, F. *Poética II, poemas de Alberto Caeiro*. Porto Alegre: L&PM, 2006.

Pirandello, L. *Right You Are, If You Think You Are*. New York: Dover Thrift, 1ª Edição, 1997.

Ricoeur, P. *La Methaphore vive*. Paris: Seuil, 1975.

Rosa, J. *Grande Sertão: Veredas*. Rio de Janeiro: Nova Aguilar, 1995.

Rotterdam, E. *Elogio da Loucura*. São Paulo: Atena, 8ª edição, 2002.

Cervantes Saavedra, M. *O Engenhoso fidalgo D. Quixote de La Mancha*. Belo Horizonte: Itatiaia, 4ª edição, 1997.

Szondi, P. *Ensaio Sobre o Trágico*. Rio de Janeiro: Jorge Zahar, 2004.

Twain, M. *Pudd'nhead Wilson And Those Extraordinary Twins*. New York: Barnes & Noble, 2005.

Trigale, D. *A arte poética de Horácio*. São Paulo: Musa Editora, 1993.

Voltaire. *Cândido Ou o Otimismo*. Porto Alegre: L&PM, 1998.

www.ingramcontent.com/pod-product-compliance
Lightning Source LLC
Chambersburg PA
CBHW031455040426
42444CB00007B/1109